[redacted]

[redacted]

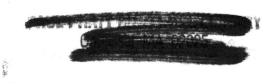

FROM **CLOTH** TO
AMERICAN FLAG

by Melanie Mitchell

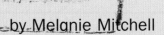 Lerner Publications Company / Minneapolis

Lerner Publications Company
A division of Lerner Publishing Group
241 First Avenue North
Minneapolis, MN 55401 U.S.A.

Website address: www.lernerbooks.com

Library of Congress Cataloging-in-Publication Data

Mitchell, Melanie S.
    From cloth to American flag / by Melanie Mitchell; photographs by Lynn Stone.
        p.   cm. — (Start to finish)
    Includes index.
    Summary: Follows the making of an American flag from the weaving of thread into cloth to the completed banner flying in the wind.
    ISBN: 0–8225–1386–2 (lib. bdg. : alk. paper)
    1. Flags—United States—Juvenile literature.
    [1. Flags—United States.] I. Title. II. Start to finish (Minneapolis, Minn.)
    CR113.M5185 2004
    929.9'2'0973—dc21   2003009054

Manufactured in the United States of America
1 2 3 4 5 6 – DP – 09 08 07 06 05 04

All photographs appear courtesy of Lynn Stone, with the exception of the following images: Corbis Royalty Free Images, cover; Photodisc, pp. 1 (bottom), 3, 23; © Bill Barley/SuperStock, p. 5; © Owen Franken/CORBIS, p. 7.

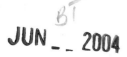
Table of Contents

Look! An American flag!

How is a flag made?

Machines make cloth.

American flags are made from cloth. Cloth is made on **looms.** Looms are machines that weave thread into cloth.

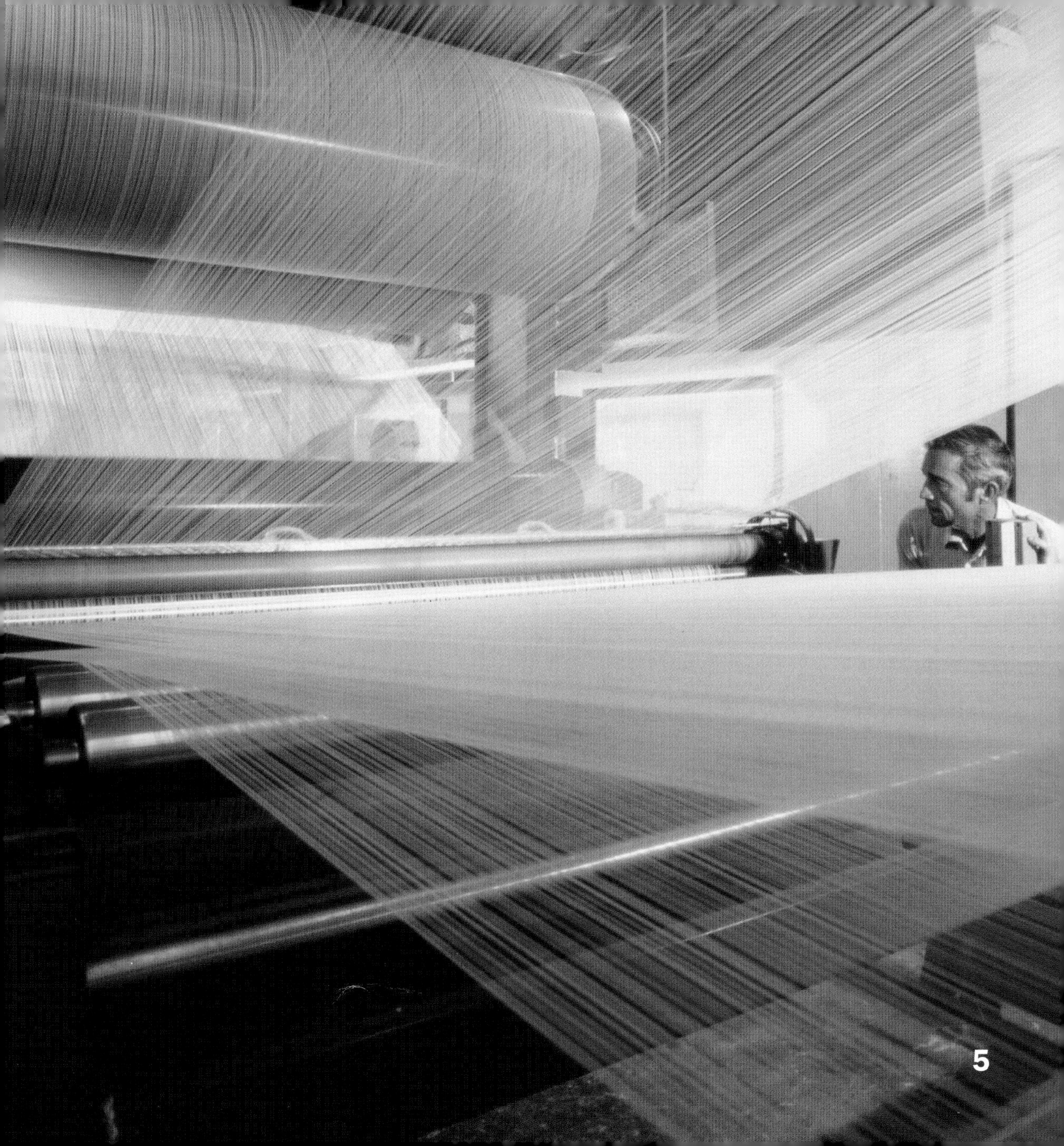

The cloth is colored.

Workers dip cloth into **dye.** Dye is a liquid that colors the cloth. American flags need red, white, and blue cloth. The wet cloth is put on a rack to dry. Then the cloth is sent to a **factory** where American flags are made.

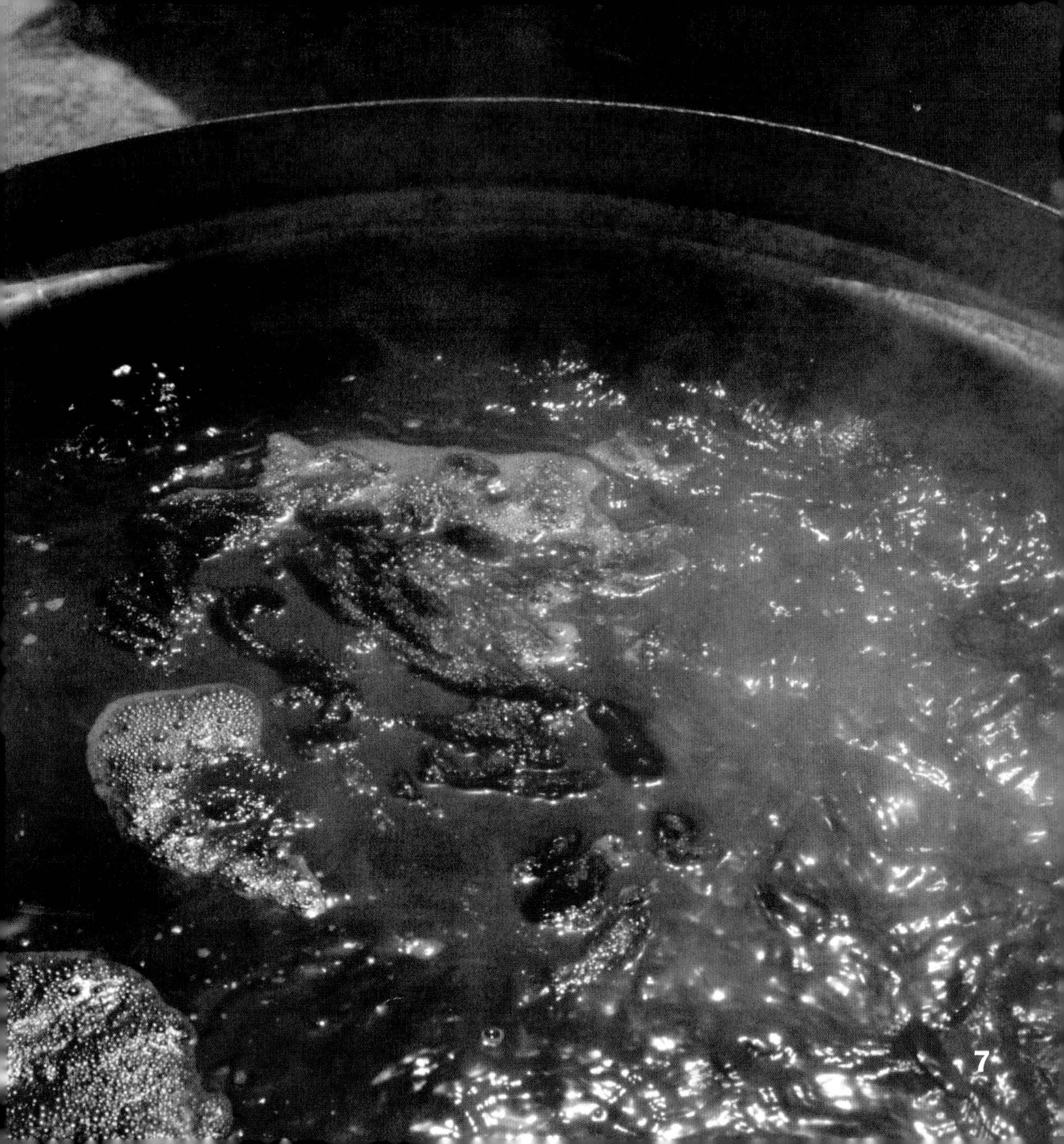

Strips are cut.

Workers cut **strips** of red and white cloth for the flags. Strips are long, skinny pieces of cloth. These strips are used to make stripes for the flags. Every American flag has 13 stripes.

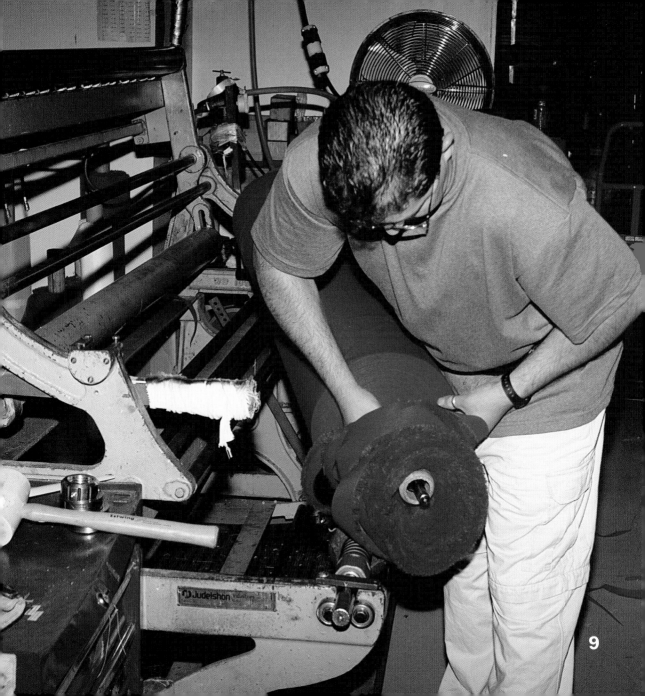

The stripes are sewn.

Large sewing machines sew the stripes together. There are 7 red stripes and 6 white stripes on each flag. Every flag has a red stripe on the top and a red stripe on the bottom.

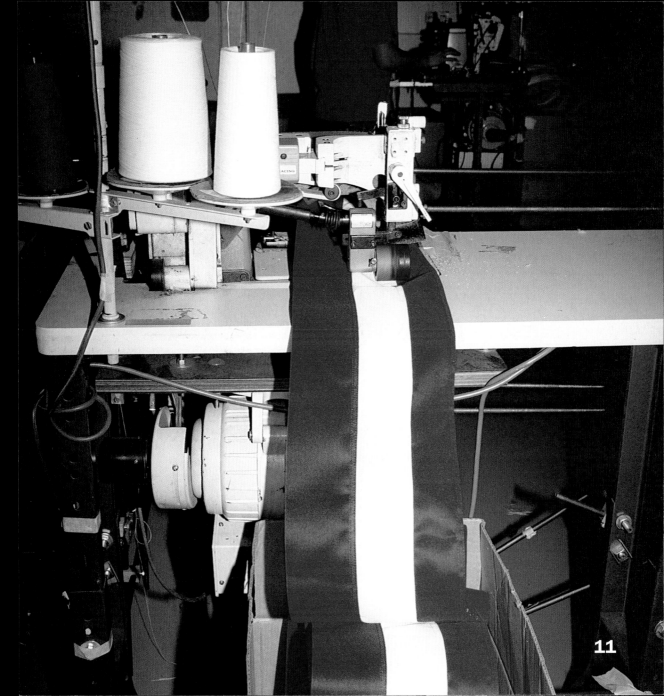

11

Blue squares are cut.

Blue cloth is cut into many squares. Each American flag has one blue square.

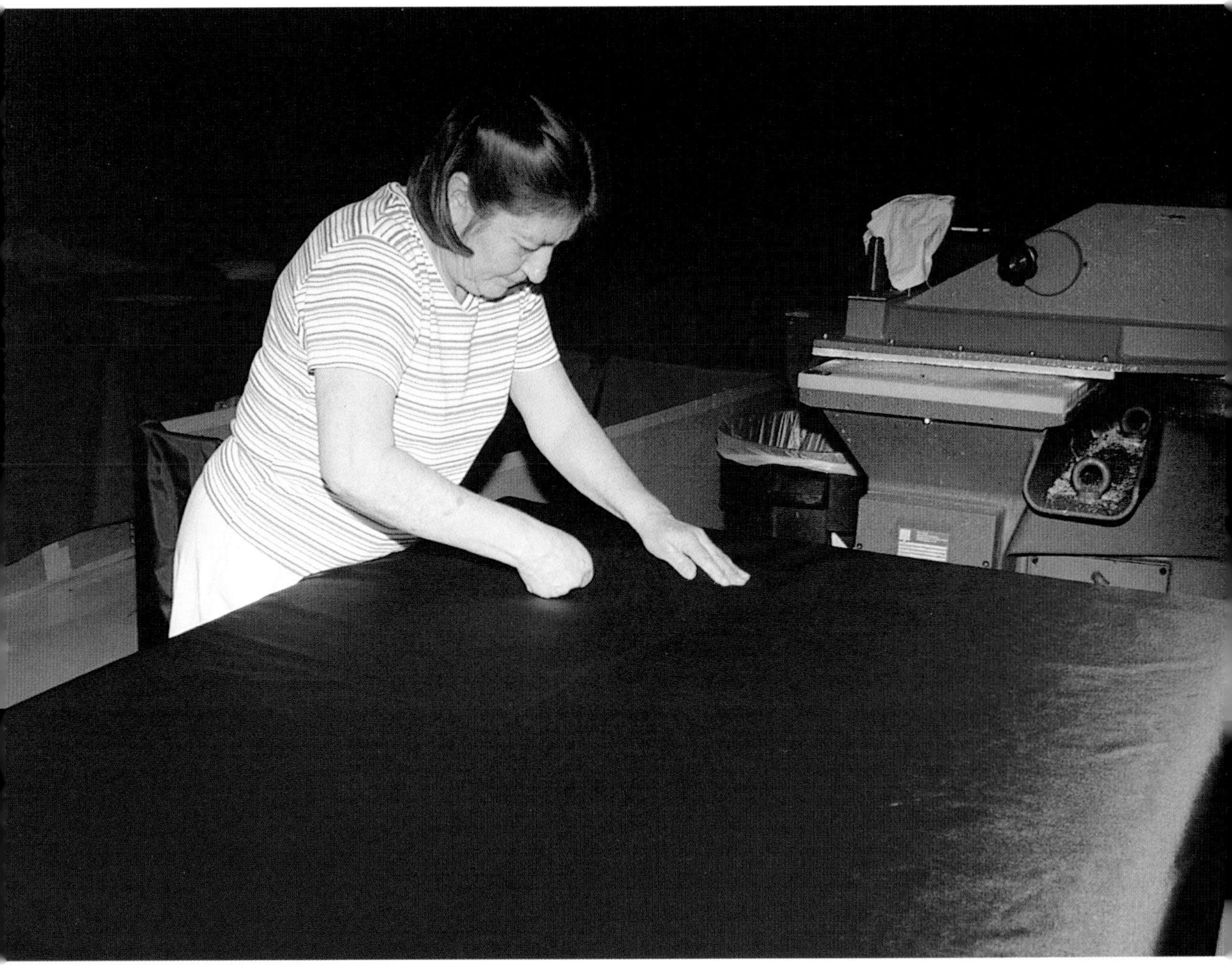

Stars are cut.

Workers cut stars from white cloth. There are 50 stars on each American flag. Each star stands for one of the 50 states in the United States.

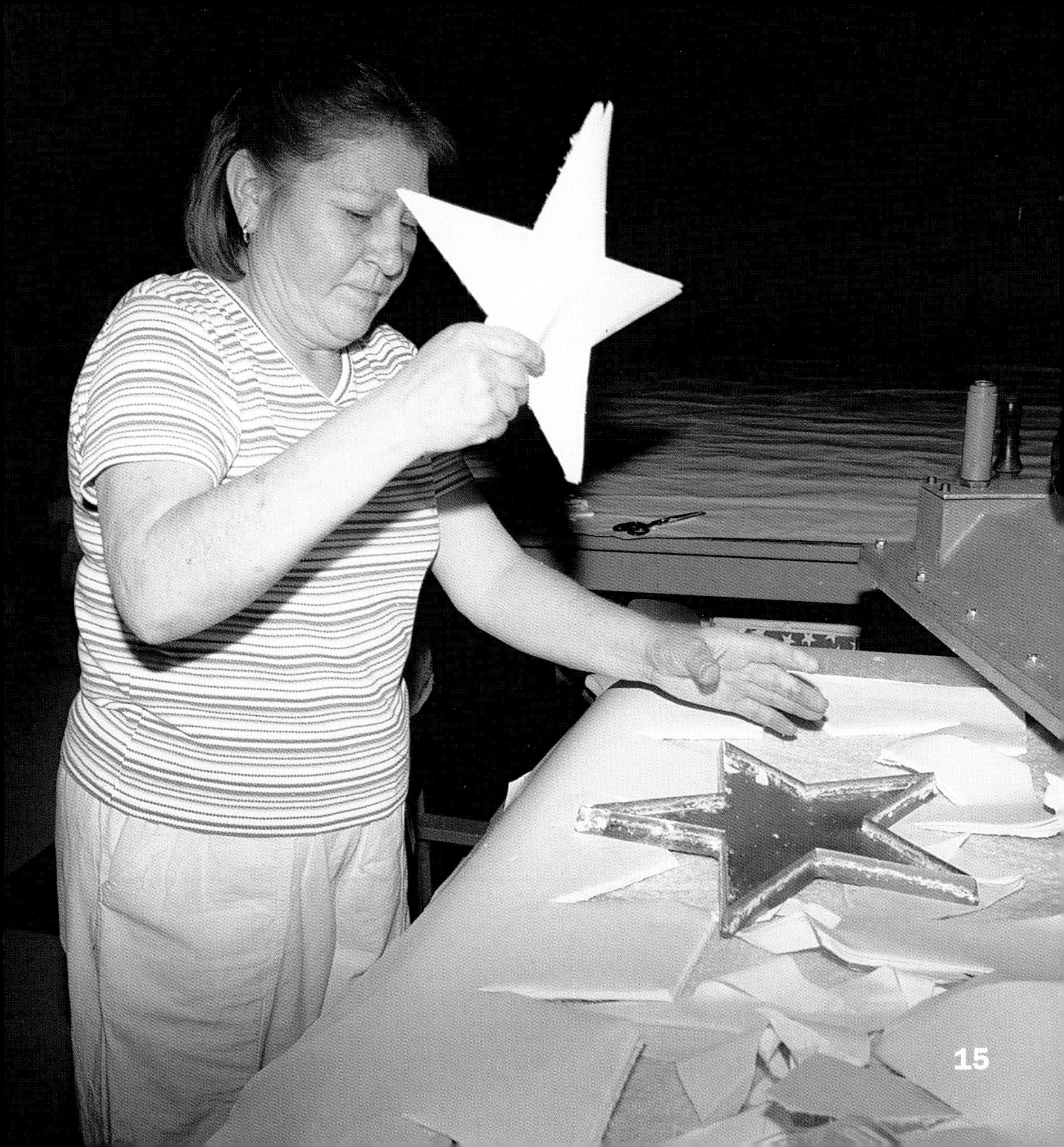

The stars are sewn.

The stars are sewn onto the blue squares of cloth. The stars can be sewn by hand or by a sewing machine. A sewing machine sews much faster than a person sews by hand.

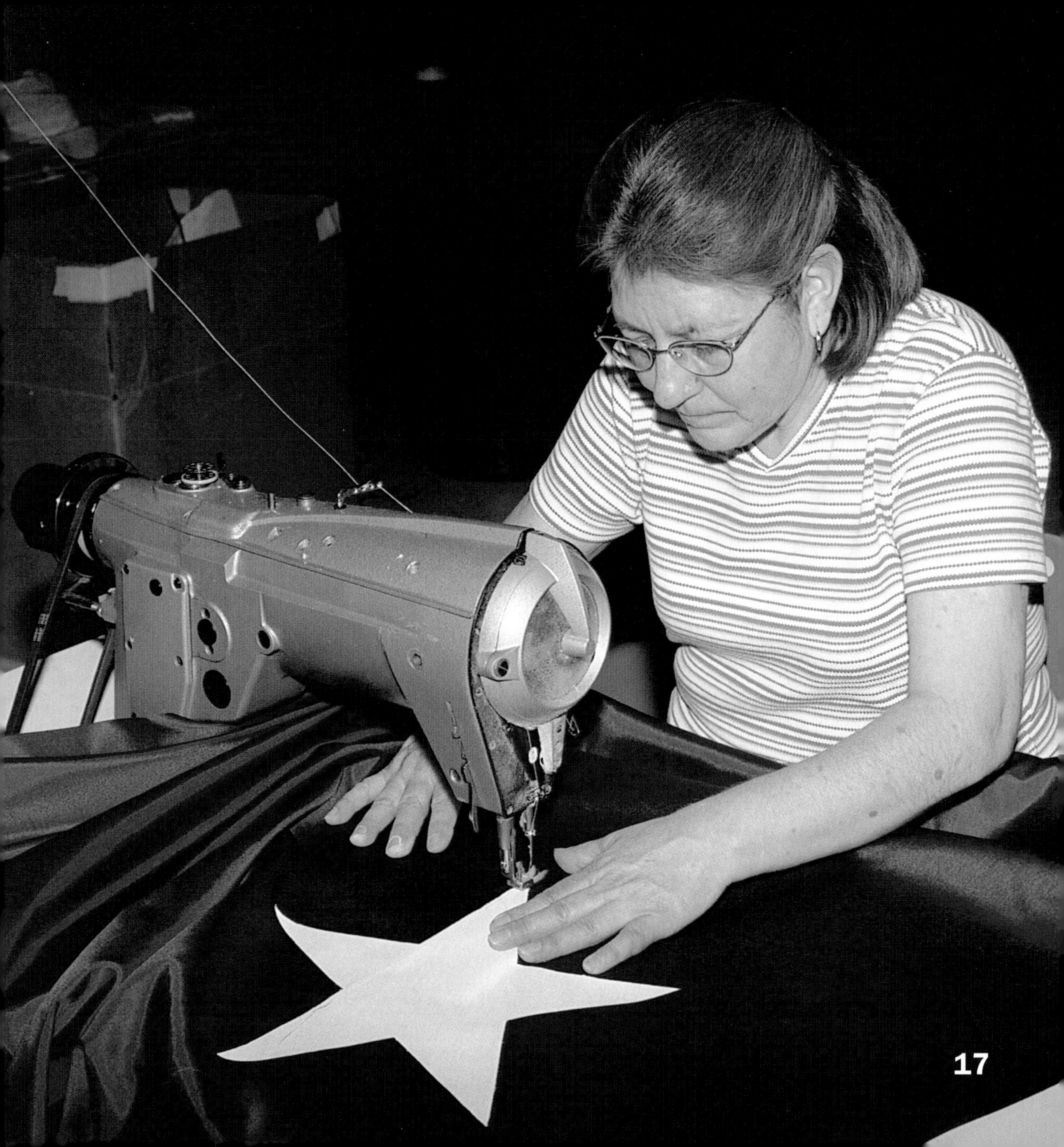

Workers sew the blue squares and stripes together.

The blue squares are sewn onto the upper left corner of the stripes. The flags are finished.

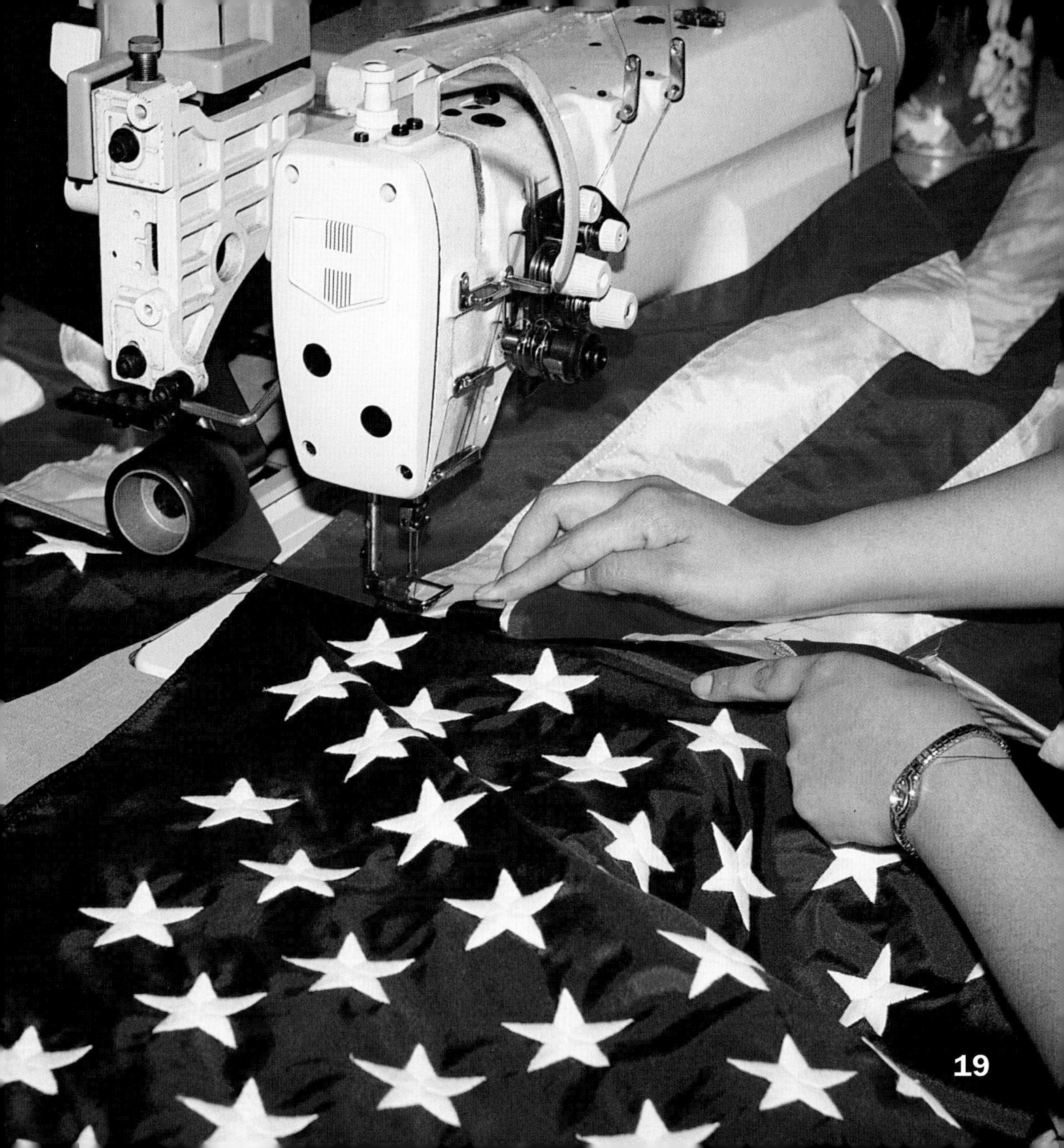

The flags are wrapped.

The new flags are folded and wrapped. Trucks take the flags to stores to be sold. People buy the flags to fly or wave.

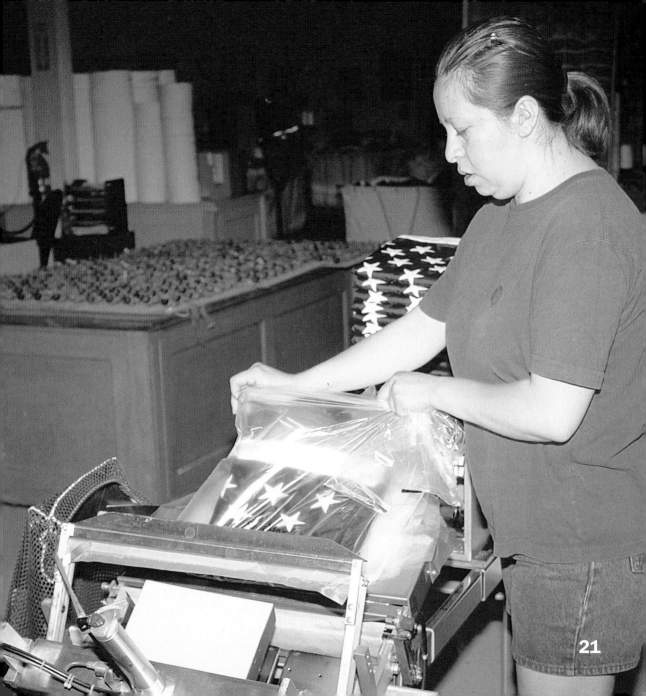

American flags fly in the wind!

People fly American flags to show that they are proud of their country. Where do you see American flags flying?

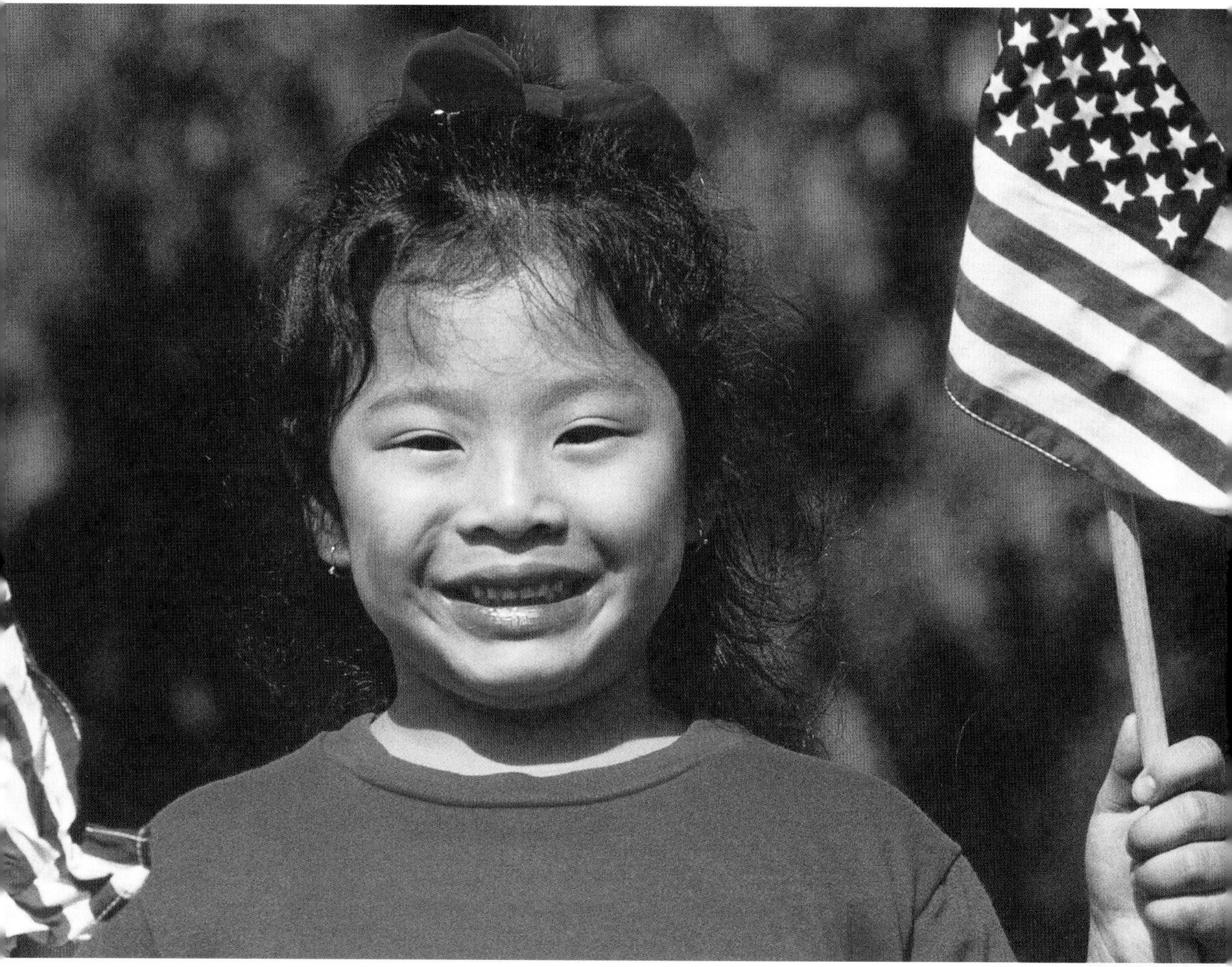

Glossary

dye (DY): a liquid used to change the color of cloth

factory (FAK-tur-ee): a place where things are made

looms (LOOMS): machines that weave thread into cloth

strips (STRIHPS): long, skinny pieces of cloth

Index